thoughts
on the road to iona

Fr JIM BYERS

thoughts on the Road to íona

ST PAULS

Illustrated by Pat Edwards

ST PAULS
Morpeth Terrace, London SW1P 1EP, U.K.

Set by TuKan, High Wycombe
Produced in the EC
Printed by The Guernsey Press Co. Ltd., Guernsey, C.I.

ST PAULS is an activity of the priests and brothers
of the Society of St Paul who proclaim the Gospel
through the media of social communication

table of contents

Dedication

Dedicated to my family and friends and all who have supported and encouraged me and prayed for me in all my ventures.
A special word of thanks to the Contemplatives of the Good Shepherd in Manchester (and formerly in Bishopton) whose prayers for me are such a source of strength. And not least to Phyllis Barrett whose determination that the spoken word of reflections on radio become the written word of this booklet. God bless you all.

íntroduction

Since the coming of local radio to west-central
Scotland 25 years ago, I have been involved on a
fairly regular basis in presenting either the
'Morning Thought' or 'Time Out' just before the
midnight news. There's always the challenge, not
only of finding something to say, but of saying it
effectively in only one minute. When I was asked
to put some of the short thoughts and reflections
in book form I found that even more of a
challenge. There is a great gulf between the
spoken word and the written word. I was worried
that what might sound fine on radio, with voice
and particular inflection, may not have the same
power or meaning in written form. That is left to
the reader. And what of the format and plan of the
thoughts in book form? With the coming of the
new Millennium I found a possible format for the
thoughts. We are about to celebrate 2000 years of
Christianity and the beautiful island of Iona is the
Cradle of Christianity for Scotland with the coming
of St Columba in 563. A few years ago I was
involved in a six week television series, 'The Road

to Iona' for the BBC. It followed a pilgrim journey from Glasgow to Iona over six weeks and was a wonderful experience of the journey of faith. And so the title for these reflections, Thoughts on the Road to Iona. Hopefully they will help you in some small way to reflect on the daily challenge of the journey of faith – in relation to God – in relation to those we encounter on life's journey – in relation to ourselves.

Jim Byers

pneuma

The wind did blow the gale blew fierce;
with resistance strong I battled on.
My head bowed low, my body arched;
perseverance bold opposed the cold.
And then a quiet sheltered glade,
made me hide in shelter and shade.
I looked at wind, so strong, so wild,
and then a seagull like a child
floated high, then soared above.

What is this wind this power so wild,
that makes me fight that finds me cowered?
The wind so strong by me resisted,
the seagull's flight is sure assisted.
It floats on wings in hovering space,
uses the wind so full of grace.

And then I think of that wind strong,
of my resistance – oh so wrong.
The wind, the Spirit are but one,
to use it, right, to fight it, wrong.

So, teach me, Lord, your Spirit's song,
to use and float and thus be strong.
And when in stubbornness I resist You
bend me, don't break me
thus love and awake me.

week 1

sunday

There's a great story told of the tourist who asked for directions in a remote part of the south west of Ireland. Having thought for a while on the problems of reaching the destination requested, the local Irish gent began, "Sure, if I were you, I wouldn't want to start from here". A beautiful and very simplistic attitude. "I wouldn't want to start from here." But the reality is that on any journey, especially a pilgrimage of faith, the only starting point can be where we are at the present moment – as we are, how we are, who we are. We begin by accepting the reality of our situation. The destination is marked out. The challenge is not wishing our starting point were somewhere else. God accepts us where we are – not where we'd rather be. Columba's journey to Iona was a real challenge of faith. He left the security of his home and entrusted the direction of his journey to God. As we start this journey, this pilgrimage of faith, we begin where we are in life and, like Columba, like Abraham (our father in faith), entrust ourselves and our journey to God, The starting point is ME – the destination is closer Union with God.

monday

Over the past few months I haven't managed to keep up my fitness programme as I used to. I used to be a regular at running and swimming to keep me fit for hill walking. You let the training slip and the fitness quickly goes. What's worse is trying to get back into it again. Back to the training – getting the body going. It's difficult, but well worth the effort. They say it's by the pain that you gain. Ouch!

St Paul likens the journey through life to union with God to a race and a group of athletes in training. We need to keep fit, to persevere, to keep running to the end. But, as with physical fitness it's easy to let faith slip. The training goes by the way. "I used to go to church" – "to pray" – "to believe". "It was good – it gave peace and inner strength". I wonder how many can say that? We have to believe that it's never too late to start. So, today, why not get into the faith training programme again. Just talk to God in your own words. Prayer is simply the raising of mind and heart to God.

tuesday

The billboards proclaim it – "Opening August". Next month – next week! The question and prayer on thousands of lips is, "Will it? Won't it?" The hope is for an end to delay and frustration. For months – for years it's been going on – so much annoyance – so much frustration – and no doubt eventually a mere resignation to the reality and frustration. But the Billboards proclaim "Completion August". And what is it? It's the road works at the big Interchange near my house. Daily hold ups, traffic jams and frustration. But day and daily a designer's plan has been unfolding as new roads and flyovers develop. A little change here and there and now with bated breath people hope that the promise of an August completion will be fulfilled. A plan unfolding and a promise fulfilled. It could be compared with God's plan and God's promise. We are all part of the plan. But only if we play our part in the unfolding of that plan, only by living out the plan or the commandment of love, will we see God's promise for us fulfilled.

wednesday

I remember hearing of an archaeologist
investigating a tomb in one of the great
pyramids. In one of the burial chambers he
found a small bowl with some seeds in it.
They were, no doubt, for the buried Pharaoh
to plant in the next life. The seeds were
thousands of years old. Out of curiosity the
archaeologist took some of the seeds from
the pyramid, planted them in soil and
watered them. A matter of days later he saw
the first tiny shoots of plants rising from the
soil. Amazing! The seeds were thousands of
years old, yet in the right conditions of soil
and sun and water their potential for growth
and life was there. In Scripture, God's word
is compared to a seed. Real life only comes
if the right conditions for growth and life are
present. Each one of us is asked to be the
soil, the sun and the water that allows God's
word and His Kingdom to grow.

thursday

I'm sure every one of us has a morning routine that we try and stick to. Its regularity helps to break us gently into the reality of a new day. I'm a diabetic of long standing. Part of my morning routine is an injection of insulin. Another part of my morning routine is to do a blood test. It's amazing how a blood test can give you a kind of MOT on the condition and health of your body. Doctors regularly take blood samples from patients to find out their real condition. Like a blood test, faith asks us to look honestly into ourselves and see the condition we are in in relation to God, to those around us and to ourselves. After a blood test the doctor may give a prescription for improving health and well being. God, too, gives a prescription – a prescription for eternal life and happiness: Love God, love your neighbour, love yourself. How is your faith blood test today?

fRíday

One of the essentials of going on holiday is luggage. I hate packing. Always the question – what to take and what to leave. Invariably you decide to take everything but the kitchen sink – then discover the limitations of a suitcase. But there are all the questions – the needs for the journey – the weather conditions, good or bad. Better being prepared. How much will a suitcase hold? Invariably we end up with a lot more baggage than we need. And I suppose we can even compare all that to life itself and to life's journey. Like packing for a summer holiday, every so often we need to take stock of the journey of life. Have we packed the essentials for life and life's journey or do we carry too much unnecessary baggage with us? As we go through Passport Control or Customs do we feel guilty when we have more than we should have? I suppose when it comes to life's journey the simplest list of items for the journey is found in the Ten Commandments, summed up simply in: love God, love neighbour, love self. There's enough weight in that for any journey through life.

saturday

Camped on the Island of Mull a couple of years ago while on a visit to Iona, I went to collect water – no, not from some very conveniently placed tap but rather from a stream flowing from the hillside. It reminded me of the time when I was watched by a foreign tourist while collecting stream water. He said, "You're not going to drink that," – with a look of disgust on his face. "But the pollution!" The stream water was crystal clear and as fresh and refreshing as you could want. I thought it sad and strange that nowadays so many people presume pollution, disease and infection unless it's out of a tap or sealed in a bottle. I remember years ago drinking water from the River Dee. I was at its very source as it gurgled out of the ground high in the Cairngorm mountains. Yes, as it wound and flowed to the sea it would become polluted. But close to its source it was clear, pure and beautiful. People, too, can be like water – so easily polluted. As long as we stay close to the source of real life we can be pollution free. That's why Jesus said, "I have come that they may have life and have it to the full."

week 2

sunoay

Have you ever been out, either walking or in the car or bus, in windy and wet weather and seen these people – idiots you probably think – out running? They're mad-keen on keeping fit – or perhaps just mad! I had to get that in, because I'm one of them. I managed a few runs last week in that really showery and windy weather. On one of the days I thought I was really flying along the road, then realised there was a strong wind at my back, blowing me along. You can imagine my feelings when I turned to head back – right into the teeth of the wind! Character forming? No, just energy-sapping! What really maddened me was when I looked up and saw some seagulls gracefully hovering in the self same wind I was battling against. I suppose there are many things in life you can either battle against or float along with. In Scripture one word is used to mean breath, spirit or wind. It made me think, as I ran, of how some people move with the Spirit of God and others seem to battle against the Spirit. A challenge for today and this week.*

* The Reflection 'Pneuma' at the front is based on this experience.

monday

I went out for a meal recently to a new restaurant. As I waited to order I noticed something I'd never seen anywhere else. They had a menu done in Braille for the blind. I opened it and was fascinated. Blank pages with an those raised dots. There are so many blind people, yet their sense of touch lets them feel and read, which compensates for their lack of physical sight. There are none so blind as those who will not see. We should realise there are many levels of blindness. The physically blind can use their sense of touch to feel, to see, to understand. Often each one of us can be blind, blind to the needs of those around us, at home, at work. Today, let's open our eyes, let's touch the lives of those we meet, get the feel for their needs. And didn't Jesus do that each day of his life?

tuesday

I watched a film on video a couple of weeks ago. It was called Mr Holland's Opus. It was about a gifted musician and composer. His whole life was music. He became a teacher and helped to inspire others to appreciate the wonder of music and sound. He then rejoiced at the birth of his son – someone to whom he could pass on the wonder of music. You can imagine his shock when it was discovered that his son was deaf. The man threw himself more and more into music and teaching and as his son grew up so also did the gap between the two of them. The son may have been deaf – but his dad had cut himself off from understanding or listening to his son's needs. The son was physically deaf – but his dad was also very deaf. Today, as we appreciate music and sound, let's also listen to the needs and messages that can come from people all around us, people we can so easily take for granted. And didn't Jesus heal all levels of deafness?

WEDNESDAY

I managed to watch an episode of 'Birds of a Feather' on television a couple of weeks ago. Sharon and Tracy had been invited along to a school reunion. They weren't looking forward to it, but they went. Sharon started reminiscing on school days and spoke of one girl who made her life a misery, played tricks on her and always got the better of her. Sharon decided that if this girl appeared she'd give her what for and really go through her. She got all worked up and ready for battle as she heard someone mention the other girl's name. But what a change came over her when the other girl appeared – now disabled and confined to a wheelchair. Sharon lost the anger and was all nice and all sympathy. But the girl in the wheelchair was still the same person and soon was playing tricks at Sharon's expense. Today, let's respect each person's dignity by being totally open and honest and accepting – not patronising. That, too, was a great quality of Jesus.

thursday

I celebrated my 37th anniversary a couple of weeks ago. It's 37 years since I was rushed into hospital in a coma. As a 14-year-old boy I was told I had diabetes and would have to give myself daily injections of insulin to survive. It certainly didn't hold me back from doing a lot of mountaineering, running and long distance swimming. 37years later I'm on four injections of insulin each day. Besides the insulin and exercise I constantly need to know just how my body is doing – how my blood sugar is. For this I do blood tests several times each day. As a priest I often relate my lifestyle as a diabetic with my relationship to God. Like a blood test I need to take stock of my relationship with God. Like an injection I need the daily routine of conversation with God in prayer. But forget the diabetes forget the priest; surely relationship with God and routine of prayer is something we should all be looking at!

fRíðay

I remember a few years ago being on holiday and climbing high in the Austrian Alps. It was magnificent. I remember one day on the descent from a mountain summit my friends and I were coming down a narrow snow covered rocky ridge. At the foot of the ridge were three climbers waiting to go up. As we came down beside them we said, "Hello!" One of them immediately piped up, "Ah, you are English!" to which one of my friends immediately replied, "No! We are Scottish!" And the response to that was "Oh, English – Scottish – it makes no difference!" To which my friend responded, "And you are German!" This brought out a fierce response. "No! We are Austrian!" And, of course, my friend's response was, "Austrian – German – it makes no difference." "Touché!" was the only response to that. A sense of identity is very important. National pride and identity certainly shows itself during events like the World Cup. Jesus also presented a sense of identity and belonging for those who would be his followers. The Christian identity was to be the Cross – but the cross itself is a sign of unconditional love. Now there's a great identity to have!

saturday

I am always fascinated when I go into the hills by the ptarmigan. It's a fascinating bird whose plumage and colour help it to blend into its background. In winter the ptarmigan is white to blend with the snow. In spring it changes colour to blend in with rock and heather. The ptarmigan's defence is not only its plumage and colour but the fact that it will stand rock still to blend into the background and not be noticed. I suppose very often we can be like the ptarmigan. We don't want to be different – we don't want to be noticed – we'd rather just stand still and blend into the background – no matter what that background may be. But do we still do the same if that background is one of injustice or something we believe to be wrong? Jesus was no ptarmigan! He didn't just blend in. Not him! A crucifixion doesn't blend in. He doesn't expect his followers to blend in either.

week 3

sunday

As we come to this third week on the
journey of faith we need to be affirmed in
our direction through faith. I remember a
few years ago bringing in the New Year with
a friend on a mountain near Arrochar. It was
a cold, cloudless night. Far from city lights,
the darkness was extreme and the cloudless
sky allowed the stars in their millions to
shine. We put up our tent high in the hills
and just stood outside staring at the vastness
of the universe in the millions of stars. I can
honestly say that in the vastness of time and
space and in the darkness of that mountain I
felt very small and totally insignificant. But
then I reflected on the Christmas we had just
celebrated. I remembered that in the
vastness of time and space Christmas is God
telling me he loves me – personally,
infinitely, unconditionally. At this thought I
no longer felt small and insignificant. Later
that night, curled up in my sleeping bag, I
awoke with a brilliant light shining through
the tent. Looking out, the whole
mountainside was illuminated by a brilliant
full moon in the cloudless sky. Then I
reflected that the moon has no light of its
own. It is merely a reflection of the sun in

another part of the sky. The full message then came home to me. As the moon reflects the brightness of the sun so I too have to reflect the light and brightness of the Son – the Son of God who came on earth and loves me. A challenge for each new week and each new day.

monday

A friend of mine recently passed his driving test. One of the first things to be done, of course, was to remove the 'L' plates from the car. I remember the day I passed my driving test over 30 years ago – I was stopped by the police within hours. The 'L' plates may have been off the car but the inexperience still showed. Thank God the police officer was understanding. As he looked at the slip of paper giving that day's date for the test pass he said something that has stayed with me ever since. He said, "You may have removed the 'L' plates but always remember you're a learner every time you get behind the wheel of a car." I remember seeing a poster with the caption: "Too much of the world is run on the theory that you don't need road manners if you're a 10-ton truck. In life we are learners every day. The road manners of life should be based on Jesus' theory: "As long as you do it to any of my brothers or sisters you do it to me."

tuesday

Crossing over to Mull last year I found the usual squad of seagulls following the ferry from Oban, hoping for some scraps and being the scavengers they seem to be. Whether on the ferry or being in Greenock as I am, there are always plenty of seagulls about. I always remember that great wee book called *Jonathan Livingston Seagull*. It's the story of a seagull that wanted to develop its gift and natural ability to fly to the very best. I always think of that story as I watch seagulls so gracefully hover, float, dive and do all kinds of aerodynamic wonders. I got really angry when some local lads used seagulls for target practice with air rifles. They killed one and injured another. The great gift of flight – the potential wasted. For each of us, too, there are gifts, talents, abilities and so often we fail to use them to our full potential. Jesus' parable of the talents shows we can do so much if we really try. And he also tells us we lose everything if we don't. So remember, "what you are is God's gift to you; what you become is your gift to God".

wednesday

It's amazing the daft things you do when you're on holiday. Last year I was camped on a remote part of the island of Mull. On one of the evenings I went the few yards from my tent down to the rocks at the water's edge. It was a beautiful evening. As I stood there on the rocks, very relaxed, I watched the tide come in. So imperceptible yet so quick. I watched the water lap then cover a shell and in minutes the rock I was standing on was an island. Twice daily the tide rises and falls – all taken for granted – all so imperceptible. Funny how we take the order of creation for granted. All too often we only take note of the order and power of creation in nature when it poses a threat to us. I often think of the passage in the Gospel when Jesus and the disciples were crossing the lake and a storm broke. Even the disciples who were fishermen and knew the waters, were scared. But Jesus calmed the storm and rebuked the disciples for their lack of faith. The challenge of real faith in practice! When storms and problems seem to threaten us do we panic – or let Jesus who calmed the storm on the lake also calm us. "A peace the world cannot give – this is my gift to you."

thursday

I remember one holiday spending some time
sailing and sea-fishing with a friend in the
Outer Hebrides. Time passed quickly and
darkness and a typical island mist seemed to
descend simultaneously – and we were still
an hour from the mooring. Undaunted by
the darkness or mist we sailed straight to the
mooring, guided all the way through the
wonder of the boat's radar system. Without
it there would have been untold problems
and dangers difficult to foresee or overcome.
Helped by the radar we managed to navigate
confidently and safely to our mooring. In
some ways faith is like radar. It helps us to
guide and navigate ourselves through life
towards our ultimate mooring in heaven.
Even when things seem to get dark and
there appear to be pitfalls all around us, faith
in God is like that radar beacon that
supports and guides us. When Thomas said
to Jesus, "Lord, we don't know where we're
going, so how can we know the way?" Jesus
answered, "I am the Way and the Truth and
the Life."

fRiDay _____

My holiday this year will be spent, weather
permitting, climbing in the Cuillins of Skye. I
love the place. I'll be climbing there with my
friend Tom. There's a lot of rock climbing
and scrambling in the Cuillins and Tom is
not used to that. Lately, I've had him away
teaching him to abseil and doing some basic
rock climbing. The first time he abseiled he
watched as I set up all the safety equipment
at the top of a cliff face. I then explained as I
showed him the equipment and the safety
harness and secured the rope then stood
him at the edge of the cliff. I then told him
to lean back over the cliff top. Slowly and
surely, with heart pounding, he leaned back.
He was totally secure. Yes, it's an unnatural
thing to do – but Tom soon learned to
understand and to trust the equipment. Trust
– a great quality! It's also the quality of faith
that helps us let go and trust God.

saturday

I recently heard a couple of old people
reminiscing about the "good old days" of
their childhood "Do you remember all those
winter pea-soupers?" asked one. "What fog!
You couldn't see the length of your arm. The
only thing that knew where to go was the
tram. Anniesland to Langside and only 10
minutes late. Follow the rails and there you
are. No bother at all!" It reminded me of the
life of a great nineteenth century English
thinker, John Henry Newman. At one stage
in his life he was very undecided about what
direction his life would take him. Crossing by
boat from Palermo to Marseilles the ship he
was on was becalmed in a thick fog. As he
stood on deck he marvelled when suddenly
the sun lazily appeared through the fog and
soon all was clear. John Henry then realised
that problems were like being in a thick fog.
Through faith and trust, God would lead
through and so he penned the prayer, "Lead
kindly light amid the encircling gloom. Lead
thou me on." So often in life we can lose a
sense of direction and purpose – all fogged
in. That's when we need real faith in Jesus
who is the light of the world.

week 4

sunday

A few years ago I joined that increasing throng of people who go running. I remember my first 15-mile run with Gerry, who was always so full of chat and encouragement. By the 13-mile stage I must admit to feeling exhausted. Then Gerry asked, "Have you ever read that prayer called 'Footprints'?" I wasn't quite up to conversation, so Gerry continued "It's all about this man talking to God at the end of his life. He's shown his journey through life as a set of footprints in the sand. And almost all the way through there's a second set of footprints – they belonged to God, who always walked beside the man. But every so often, at the really hard times in his life, the man noticed there was only one set of footprints. "Typical of you, God," he said, "left me on my own just when I needed you." God's answer was perfect. He said, "Those difficult times when you see only one set of footprints – that's when I carried you." As I then reached the 14-mile mark I realised I too was being carried, supported and encouraged by Gerry and his timely tale – but more probably by God, who uses Gerry and you and me to support others.

monday

They say that the mind is like a parachute –
it works only when it's open. I've always
longed to do a parachute jump. The
freedom, the thrill of seeing the canopy
open and fill with air as you descend. And,
of course, there's always the initial fear of
the parachute not opening. That would
more than likely mean death. But it's true
that if we're not open – to God, to people,
to growth, to change – then we're as good
as dead. When Jesus came into the world
many of the religious leaders had stopped
letting their minds be open and filled with
the wonder of God. They had reduced God
to a mere set of restrictive and narrow rules
– poor fundamentalists! Jesus came to open
their minds and hearts to the expanse of
God's love. Closed minds didn't accept him
and died. Open minds did accept him and
found life. Yes, real faith has to be like a
parachute. It works only when it's open.

tuesday

They say you can either complain because rose bushes have thorns or rejoice because thorn bushes have roses! Some people are never happy. Are you an optimist or a pessimist? Do you tend to see the good side of things or the bad? Do you see the best or the worst in people? If you're always being negative and pessimistic you'll never really cope with the challenge of life. Faith is something that should help us to be hopeful and positive. In the Gospels there are many incidents where people might seem to have every night to be negative and pessimistic – the sick, the crippled, the weak, the sinners. But they presented themselves to Jesus in all their weakness and need – and found healing, strength, new life and hope. So, today, start off in a positive faith. Don't complain because rose bushes have thorns – rather rejoice because thorn bushes have roses!

Wednesday

They say that to wonder is to begin to understand. They also say that "Curiosity killed the cat". But if we didn't ask questions, wonder about things, then we would never have advanced in medicine, science and technology. A child keeps asking questions – "What's that?" "Why?" and so on. By asking questions, by wondering we learn and we understand The whole wonder of creation lies all around us. It has a form, as regular as the seasons of the year, as fascinating as growing crystals. Throughout our lives we should be filled with wonder, and all that wonder should help us appreciate more and more God the Creator. And it's only at the end of life here on earth that we shall fully understand, because then we shall have before us not just creation but the Creator. Then we will fully understand. But, until then, open your eyes wide, look, and wonder.

thursday

They say that "Happiness is a direction – not a place." People very often like to use their imagination to dream of what would make them really happy. Usually you hear of winning the lottery, or having a big house or a luxury holiday. Yet, all too often people with all the material world has to offer are far from happy and are often very lonely. That's why we think of happiness as a direction and not a place. It starts within us, grows within us, grows as we grow. Happiness is found in the way we live. That's why in the *Sermon on the Mount* Jesus gives us the Beatitudes in terms of real happiness. "Happy are the poor in spirit... Happy the gentle... and so on. In all the Beatitudes Jesus presents us with the qualities, the characteristics of happiness. And if we look at the Beatitudes we find that these are the very qualities and characteristics of Jesus himself. True happiness, then, is found in following Jesus.

friday

In life, every day is a new experience, a new challenge. There are times when we are presented with challenges and we say, "No! I can't" And we turn away. Doing that we don't learn. We don't overcome challenges by turning away from them. We should all erase "can't" from our vocabulary. Jesus came into our world with a great gift and promise of eternal life. But just think, to fulfil that mission Jesus had to face his passion and death. In the garden of Gethsemane he was afraid and he prayed to the Father. If Jesus had not faced the challenge of his passion and death with all that entailed, then nothing would have been achieved, nothing would have changed. So, we learn from Jesus that nothing can be changed until it is faced. Challenges are often difficult. Never say, "I can't" Always say, "I'll try."

saturday

Have you ever opened a Corn Flakes box, looked inside and thought, "I've been done!" There you have this big box and you look inside and the contents only seem to fill half the box Then you look at the side of the box and find the word, "Contents may settle after packaging." Often you buy goods by the size of the packaging and expect to get them full instead of half a packet You feel done! I wonder, today, if any person will feel done having spent time with us. Jesus once said, "Give and there will be gifts for you: a full measure, pressed down, shaken together and running over will be poured into your lap; because the amount you measure out is the amount you will be given back." Each of us is a package, the Temple of God, made in His likeness. Like the Corn Flakes box do we give disappointment, or are we, in Jesus' words, ". . . a full measure, pressed down, shaken together and running over?'

week 5

I remember my brother Joseph once saying to me he was getting a bit fed up. "What's the problem?" I asked. With a grin on his face he told me he was fed up meeting people who would then ask him, "Are you Fr Jim Byers' brother?" So he now had the solution. When asked if he is my brother he answers, "No," and then adds, "Jim's my brother." A sense of personal identity is very important for each of us. I'm sure many people get fed up being identified not for themselves and their own worth, but identified in relation to someone else – Jim's brother, Joe's wife, the assistant manager, the boss's secretary. There are many examples. One of the great qualities we should learn from Jesus was his willingness to give his undivided time and attention to each person he met. His interest was in each individual. As we at times wrestle with personal identity and worth it's good to think that Jesus, speaking of our worth, said, "Why, even the hairs of your head have been counted."

monday

After a set of exams a teacher decided to speak to each pupil in the class individually. It just so happened that the pupil who got top marks and the pupil who got lowest marks were to go in one after the other. While waiting outside, the pupil with the top marks tried to upset the other pupil by saying he would get a row for his low marks. As it happened, it was the one with the top marks who came from the teachers room in tears and the one with the low marks who was all smiles. The reason? The pupil with the top marks was capable of getting even better marks than he did – but he didn't work – he didn't use his talents to the full, and so he got into trouble. The pupil with the poor marks had tried his best and worked as hard as he could and for this he was praised. God has given each of us talents. But what is important is not where we end up in any work or social scale. What is important is that we use our talents to the full. We can give no more. God can expect no less.

tuesday

I was at Killin in Perthshire a couple of weeks ago. With all the rainfall the famous falls of Dochart were a sight to see. I love the noise and turbulence of water as it jumps and tumbles and falls back on itself in white water activity. Once over the falls the water drops into a deeper, quiet and peaceful state – less dramatic and exciting. They say, "Still waters run deep." Perhaps another idea might be, "Empty vessels make the most noise." It follows! Turbulent, noisy rapids are generally very shallow. Still waters are deeper. And there's a lesson too about life and about people. Often, people that seem noisy, turbulent, spectacular and dramatic are only so on the outside – they have no real depth. Bullies and hard men act this way. But people with greater depth don't need to make a lot of noise or show to be effective. We can just think of the example of Jesus. Was he noisy or turbulent? No! "still waters run deep."

They say it's easy to be an angel when
nobody ruffles your feathers. It's true, isn't
it? When everything is going well for you
and everyone seems to be on your side life
can be quite good and straightforward. But
then things turn a bit rough. People don't
agree with you, rub you up the wrong way.
The patience soon goes, especially if
someone points out faults or areas in life
where we could improve. When Jesus began
his public life the religious leaders of the time
were quite happy. They had everything their
own way – nobody ruffled their feathers. But
then Jesus presented the teaching of God in
a way that did ruffle their feathers. As we
continue this faith journey are we willing to
accept that Jesus' teaching might ruffle our
feathers? Do we get angry or do we allow
his influence to change us? The religious
leaders of Jesus' time had closed minds.
Jesus' followers were open and receptive. To
them Jesus gave the gift of life. Let's open
our minds to Jesus today.

thursday

I met a group of ladies recently, and after introducing myself, one of the ladies said, "Wait a minute! You're the priest I've heard on Radio Clyde's Morning Thought" Then there was a pause before she said, "I never thought you looked like that. Well, what can you say? How do you react to that? We use our imagination so much – and so often our image and the reality are poles apart. I suppose Jesus, as Messiah, had the same reaction from people in his day. But, really, today is his day too, so how do we react when we meet Jesus? We might then say that we've never met him. But didn't he say, "I was hungry, I was thirsty, I was in need. Did you come to my help?" Meeting, recognising and responding to Jesus in our midst is a daily challenge for all of us. Like the lady who heard me on radio then saw me, perhaps when we meet Jesus at judgement we'll recognise someone we didn't give time to and then say, "Jesus, I never thought you looked like that".

fRidAy

I've been a diabetic now for over 37 years. I estimate I've given myself in excess of 40,000 injections of insulin in that time. "Be what you can be" was the slogan of one of the Health Education programmes. And that's so important "Be what you can be". And with determination and perseverance we can achieve almost anything. I remember too the great saying of the blind, deaf and dumb American girl, Helen Keller. She said, "Life is either a daring adventure or nothing." "Be what you can be," and "Life is either a daring adventure or nothing" are two great sayings! But they depend on a response from each of us. All too often we can put ourselves down, feel we can't do some things, and not even try. I believe very often that God has more faith in us than we have in ourselves. As we think today of those two sayings, "Be what you can be," and "Life is either a daring adventure or nothing," think also of one from the Bible. God says, "You are precious in my sight. I have carved you on the palm of my hand." Have faith in God – have faith in yourself.

saturday

I was talking to someone recently who was mourning the sudden death of a loved one. She told me she couldn't pray because she felt so hurt and angry with God. She was hurting all the more because she was bottling up the hurt and anger. We chatted then about prayer. It's an expression of faith and faith is about a loving relationship with God. In any loving relationship we need openness, trust and honesty. And that's true in our relationship with God. If prayer is about opening and raising mind and heart to God then we really tell God what's on our mind and in our heart. If that's hurt and anger then let it go – tell Him! That lady soon discovered a very fruitful prayer was telling God of her hurt and anger. He wants to hear us – as we are, how we really feel. That honest prayer gives peace and strength. The grieving lady discovered that.

week 6

sunday

The famous American civil rights champion, Martin Luther King, once made a speech about having a dream – a dream about equality for all, no matter what their colour or creed. Martin Luther King worked hard for that dream. But he was persecuted, threatened and eventually assassinated. He certainly paid the price for his dreams. It's always important to have dreams and ideals to strive for in life. But it's also important to realise that there's no point in having dreams unless you are willing to put hard work and effort into making those dreams come true. It's not easy. Perhaps you won't achieve the dream or the ideal you've set yourself. But to have put a lot of hard work and effort into trying is achievement in itself. This is the final week of our journey of faith. As a people of faith the most fundamental thing is for each of us to recognise, to accept and to treat each person we meet as a fellow child of God, a brother or sister of Christ.

monday

I have a great devotion to St Francis of
Assisi and a love of nature. Whenever I head
for the hills of the Highlands I look forward
to the drive north and to one particular
sight. As you leave Bridge of Orchy and
head up towards the bleakness and flatness
of Rannoch Moor you pass a huge boulder
by the side of the road. In the boulder
there's a deep crack and from the crack a
large rowan tree is growing. It's a fascinating
sight – all the more so because it's on the
edge of Rannoch Moor that can be bleak
and wild and has no trees – yet from this
most unexpected place the tree lives and
grows. Just a small amount of earth in the
crack in the rock was obviously sufficient for
the seed to take root and the tree to grow.
That sight at the edge of the road always
teaches me that even in a hostile and bleak
environment the seed that is God's Word
can also take root and grow.

tuesday

A turtle is well protected. A hard shell and a tough skin safeguard it from all kinds of enemies. But think of it, the turtle will get nowhere unless it sticks its neck out. It can't stay enclosed in its shell all the time. I suppose we are often the same. To make progress, to learn, to discover, we often have to stick our necks out and take risks. They may not be life-endangering risks, but it's not easy. In fact there are times you'd prefer to retract your neck like the turtle and disappear into your shell. Safety and protection, perhaps, but no progress, development or growth is made. Even being a follower of Jesus at times means sticking your neck out. You may feel shy or scared, but sticking your neck out helps you grow close to Jesus. And didn't he stick his neck out for you?

wednesday

I know an old man who might easily be described as 'perpetual motion'. In his late seventies, he's very young in spirit and very active. If he's not swimming he's doing odd jobs about the place; and if he's not doing odd jobs he's away at the sequence dancing or the football. His philosophy simply is, 'Better to wear out than to rust out'. Working since he was 14 years old he's kept very active since he retired. Yes, better to wear out than to rust out. If we are a people of faith then better to "wear out" in faith than to "rust out". There's a great chasm that exists between religion and faith. In our society and world there are countless people who claim religion of one denomination or another – but lack real faith in practice. For many people their so-called 'religious affiliation' is part of a culture of religion – but has little or nothing to do with a real living faith. A people of faith should be growing in the relationship that faith really is. Yes, in faith as in life – better to wear out than to rust out. And the challenge of faith in practice is the challenge of love. It also helps us appreciate that what we are is God's gift to us and what we become is our gift to God.

thursday

I love the battle that goes on each year in the world of nature; the battle between winter and spring. So what side are you on? Winter's chilly winds and squally snow showers threaten – but we all really know it's a losing battle. The darkness and death of winter gives way to the new life of spring. Daffodils blow their fanfare of golden yellow in the wind; the trees begin to blossom and bud; and the birds herald dawn and spring, as they sing their early morning songs and build their nests. Yes, hope springs eternal, but spring's victory over winter's darkness and death is assured. We have a deep, unshakeable faith in this victory of life over death in nature. God asks us to go beyond that to see also victory over the darkness of sin and death through Jesus, his Son, the Resurrection and the Life. If we are a people of real faith we must be open to God speaking to us – not in remoteness but close by and in the reality of nature and life all around us.

friday

Walking along the road one day in autumn I heard the squawking sound of geese in flight. Looking up I saw the familiar arrow-head formation as a flock of geese headed South. Their instinct and nature is fascinating. They seem to have an in-built guidance system as they navigate to their destination for the winter. It's usually a long, tiring flight, yet as they go their arrow-head formation means that the bird at the head is strong. It takes its turn there before going to the back. The beating of the wings in the arrow-head formation then gives uplift and support to the birds at the rear who may be weak or tired. I suppose we often crave for those goose-like instincts in our lives. If only we knew what direction life was leading us. If only we could receive support or be a support to others in day to day life. But surely that's what our journey of faith and prayer in life is all about. In the Gospels Jesus gives us the support, the direction and the assurance we need in life as he points us to the Father: "Ask and you will receive, seek and you will find, knock and the door will be opened to you".

saturday

The first time I visited Iona was when I
took part in a television series called, "The
Road to Iona." It reflected the spread of
faith from that remote island off Mull
where St Columba established his
monastery. I was on the island filming in
February. It was wet, blowing a gale, and
the waves were crashing against the shore.
It made me wonder how the Gospel
message ever landed on Iona never mind
got off again to spread far and wide over
Scotland. Each year now I visit Iona. I was
there again not long ago. It was a beautiful
summer's day this time and I was really
amazed at the bus-loads of tourists who
had come to visit Iona. On the island there
were loads of camera-clicking people.
Why, I wondered? Is it Christian heritage?
Is it a bit of history and tradition? Is it the
grave of the late John Smith? Is it a search
for traditions, roots? We so often search
the past for meaning, purpose and
direction for the present. Perhaps St
Columba, perhaps Lord MacLeod of Iona,
perhaps John Smith all reflected the search
of Thomas the Apostle. "Lord," he said,
"we don't know where you're going so

how can we know the way?" And Jesus'
answer? "I am the Way, the Truth and
the Life."